MAKING A MARRIAGE

HOW TWO BECOME ONE

Elsie Hainz McGrath

ONE LIGUORI DRIVE, LIGUORI MO, 63057-9999

Imprimi Potest:
Richard Thibodeau, C.Ss.R.
Provincial, Denver Province
The Redemptorists

ISBN 0-7648–0893-1
Library of Congress Catalog Number: 2002108165

Liguori Lifespan is an imprint of Liguori Publications.

Scripture quotations are from the *New Revised Standard Version of the Bible*, copyright © 1989 by the Division of Christian Education of the National Council of Churches of Christ in the USA. Used with permission. All rights reserved.

To order, call 1-800-325-9521
www.liguori.org
www.catholicbooksonline.com

In memory of Jim,
I dedicate these thoughts to all
engaged couples, and to married couples
who are searching for "oneness" in the days
and nights of their earthly lives. May your
marriage be a sacrament for as long
as you both shall live.

Remembrance is
a form of meeting, and I meet you often.

Kahlil Gibran

CONTENTS

Preface – 7

PART I
CATHOLICS AND MARRIAGE

Against the Odds 11

Typical Problem Area – 12

Communicaton – 16

Commitment – 19

Conflict Resolution – 20

Children – 22

Church – 24

Career– 26

Remembrance – 27

The Primacy of Persons – 29

PART II

THE WEDDING DOWRY

My Personal Baggage 31

The Physical – 33

The Emotional – 35

The Sexual – 38

The Spiritual – 41

The Sacramental – 43

PART III

THE MARRIAGE COVENANT

Two Become One 49

One Flesh – 53

For Better or Worse – 55

For Richer or Poorer – 56

In Sickness and In Health – 57

The Decision to Love – 58

Until Death – 62

PREFACE

I was a wife at 17, a mother at 18, a grandmother at 38, a great-grandmother at 58, and a widow at 59. My husband and I had been legally and validly married for forty-two years when he died. We had spawned and raised four children into adulthood and their own marriages, and had watched our immediate family expand through the addition of twelve grandchildren and one great-grandchild. And we had been happy together. But our "sacrament" of marriage had not spanned forty-two years; it had, in fact, "only just begun" twenty-four years before it ended.

In effect, it began with a fight—not an uncommon beginning to many things in our lives back then. We'd been invited to participate in a *Marriage Encounter* weekend because, according to the couple who asked us, we had "a good marriage." And from all outward appearances, we did. We'd made a pact, years earlier, to *never* reveal to others that our togetherness was a put-on. So when this invitation was made, my husband was quick to say "yes," we'd go—and I was reduced to silence. Until we were safely back in the privacy of our own home.

"What do you mean, we'll go!?! Do you want the

whole world to find out that we don't have a good marriage? You call Jerry back and tell him we can't make it!"

Ultimately, as was usually the case in those days, my husband "won" the fight. We went on the weekend that was destined to change our lives and the lives of countless others. We learned the "secret" of love—that it is a decision, not an emotion—and we decided to make our marriage the sacrament that the Church had named it.

In our remaining twenty-four years together, we lived and breathed marriage. We even attempted to "teach" it to engaged couples. Our vocation spilled over into an avocation: helping couples who were just beginning their lives together to bypass the pain and bitterness that we had lived with in our early years together. We wanted everyone to know the blessed beauty of sacramental love, becoming advocates of common marriage policies that were just beginning to take shape in dioceses around the country, and helping to initiate programs for marriage preparation which would be a required part of every common marriage policy.

For many years, we thought our efforts were successful. We touched many lives—boxes of cards and letters "prove" that. But in the end we were left with more questions than answers. Why are only half of our own children even nominally Catholic? Why are nearly half of our grandchildren unbaptized and unchurched? Why are so many couples we worked with divorced? How many of those we "taught" are also divorced? Is there something we could have done or should have done differently? Is there anything that *anybody* can really do to "teach" another person to "be sacrament"?

There are still no answers to these questions, but the desire to pass on hard-learned wisdom remains. It is my hope that this small book does that.

PART I

CATHOLICS AND MARRIAGE

Against the Odds

When I fall in love, it will be forever...." But how often *is* it forever? How can we *know* it will be? How—as we used to ask our mother—do we *know* this is really love? Oftentimes it isn't, really. Then what? Do we walk away from it...forget the promises we made...admit defeat and let all those witnesses—the Church—down? Do we "do our part" to reinforce the notion that is so prevalent in today's world, that monogamy and faithfulness is a "thing of the past"? Or do we "tough it out"— for the sake of the others, if nothing else—and *make the decision to love?* OK, so your spouse isn't "the greatest thing since sliced bread" after all. Are you?

When we were kids and we got into a fight with our "best friend," what did we do? Chances are, after a few hours or a few days, we "made up." Perhaps we *still* thought our friend was at fault in our fight, but we were willing to "let it go" for the sake of the friendship. We didn't realize it then, of course, but what we were really doing was making a decision to love our friend because we missed that part of our life that we had shared with him or her.

Certainly as teenagers, we often were "on the outs" with our mother or father. Possibly, depending upon circumstances and our own raging emotions, one or another of these fights lasted months or even years, but most of us eventually effected a reconciliation with our parents. As we got older, we realized our own earlier folly and recognized our parents always had our best interests at heart. We decided to love them, even if only for the sake of the relationship and the future of the family we are inexorably bound to.

Why, then, do some of us find it so preposterous to "decide" to love the one person in all the world who is, or was, the most important to us? We talk of "falling in" and "falling out" of love as if we have no control over these things. We say that love is a "feeling," and we can't help our feelings. We hold on to our grudges until they eventually consume us, and then we say it's "over." We decide, in other words, *not* to love: we "harden our heart" against our beloved.

Typical Problem Areas

A recent Creighton University survey revealed some startling statistics surrounding problem areas in the lives of Catholic newlyweds. These statistics are startling for two reasons: first, because Catholics have been required to participate in a marriage preparation program for the last fifteen or twenty years, at which these kinds of problems are extensively addressed; and second, because many of these couples have already "experimented" with cohabitation before marriage, one "purpose" being to "test" their compatibility before committing to a permanent relationship.

These are the dismal findings of Creighton's Center for Marriage and Family:

- seventy-nine percent of couples are wrestling with problems over expectations about household tasks
- seventy-seven percent are experiencing problems surrounding the frequency of sex
- seventy-five percent are having difficulties in balancing job and family
- seventy-two percent are fighting over their financial situation

There are endless surveys, conducted by endless organizations, which all give very similar and universally disturbing news about the plight of marriage. The divorce rate stands at roughly fifty percent for first marriages, higher for second marriages, regardless of faith or lack of it. Living together outside of marriage is on the upswing, and those who marry after having cohabitated divorce at even greater numbers than the fifty percent overall average. Yet, despite these dismal statistics, it is predicted that fully ninety percent of Americans will marry at least once and, perhaps more surprising, that those with the *most* education are the most likely to wed.

Further good news for education: the best educated are the least likely to divorce.

Marital ills are becoming a prime concern in our society, both within and outside of the Church. Prisons employ a relationship enhancement program with prisoners and their spouses, US military programs are aimed at stemming divorces, and state governments are launching partnerships with religious leaders. Even the federal government is talking about marriage legislation. There are marriage preparation programs and marriage enrichment programs and marriage saving programs.

But all surveys appear to indicate that neither living together without benefit of marriage nor participating in a marriage preparation program are contributing to good marriages. This would seem to fly in the face not only of unmarried couples rationalization for cohabitation, but also of married couples' persuasive powers of teaching witness. Perhaps, however, it simply indicates that newly married couples have to learn to become "family"…have to grow into "sacrament"…have to "experience" marriage before they can model it—no matter what kind of "preparation" they've had beforehand. As any married person can tell you, "been there, done that."

The first two problems areas on the Creighton list—household tasks and frequency of sex—have to do with expectations, not facts, but their virtual inevitability does not make them insurmountable problems. And the fact is that these were a different kind of problem for couples fifty years ago than they are now—so take a deep breath, talk about your expectations, and thank God for fifty years of advances!

Chances are some things remain the same, however. The woman may no longer be expected to give up her career to become "just a housewife," but she usually will still be stuck with a disproportionate number of household tasks. The ability to plan one's family can eliminate what used to be a constant fear of pregnancy, but long hours of work and a perceived lack of spousal cooperation in the home division of labors often contribute to a wife's diminished appetite for sex.

If it happens that household tasks and sex are or become problem areas for you, what are you going to do about it? Personally, we both learned to "settle for less," and eventually decided to be comfortable with that— not a perfect solution, but one that worked for us. As we get older, we tend to care less about the tasks that seemed so important earlier; and it's a well-established fact that a woman's sexual appetite increases almost in direct proportion to a man's decreasing appetite. (We might question God about that some day!) So you could "hope for the best" and wait! But that isn't the easiest or the smartest way to resolution. It is, in fact, a non-resolution—a kind of *laissez faire* attitude about the whole situation which diminishes its importance.

There is perhaps an inevitability about the next two major problems too—that of balancing family and job, and the always changing yet ever present financial situation you find yourselves in. Money and time management are always issues, whether married or not, but when you're married the issues are doubled because two people have to come to mutual decisions regarding them. And when you have children the issues are compounded by the numbers. One thing to remember when you make decisions around time and money—or any other decisions, for that matter—is that all such decisions are temporary. Changing circumstances call for changing options and changing options call for changing decisions.

Communication

Experts claim that communication is the biggest deciding factor in any relationship working. In fact, there are some who say that the most obvious indicator of pending divorce is our tendency to avoid confrontation. There are other deciding factors, though, and any one of them may be the "biggest," depending upon the dispositions of the individuals involved. What makes communication the biggest is its central importance in the other five, which are:

- commitment
- conflict resolution
- children
- church
- career

Communication has become a buzz word, a psychoanalyzed concept that we bring into our workplace, and into our schools and prisons and other institutional settings, in order to "improve relations" for everyone's mutual benefit. Personality tools formerly known only to the professionals are suddenly familiar to everybody: "What's your Myers-Briggs?"; "Where are you on the

Enneagram?"; "How many of your siblings are older/ younger than you?" But are our relations improved? Does knowing the personality type of our nemesis make dealing with him/her easier or more successful?

Communication within the marital relationship has to be deeper than our business dealings or we might as well be married to our boss or our secretary. Essential to sacramental communication is unconditional equality of beings—an essential that is virtually unachievable anywhere but there. No wonder that all our knowledge does little to help our professional communications; no wonder, sadly, that communication is so apt to break down even in marriage. Without an unconditional equality of beings there can be no completely revealing and receiving communication.

Now, this may sound rather rudimentary to people of the twenty-first century—the kind of stuff we all learn as we're growing up bombarded with communication techniques and feel-good psychology. But, sadly, our inherent human inability to really know ourselves, and to openly and honestly share who we are with others, remains the primary (possibly the *only*) reason for alienation and divorce. It is truly the only reason for prejudice and hatred and violence and war. We may know what we're *supposed* to do, but we still *don't do it.* We're too busy preoccupying ourselves with the noise and the glamour and the get-ahead schemes of the world to "be still and listen"—listen to the voice of God within us, listen to the feelings of another, listen to our universal hunger and need for something more, something deeper and longer-lasting than what we have before us.

Nearly everyone lives with a good bit of self-deception. In coming to know ourselves, we need to look at the masks that we hide behind. In other words, what images of self do we attempt to convey to others? We project different images to different people and in different circumstances. Why? And how successful are we? In other words, how do others see us? What have friends and foes conveyed to us about ourselves? Are they seeing the person we want them to see? Indeed, how do we actually see ourselves? How closely does our self-image mesh with our masks, and with others' images of us? Can these three views be reconciled? What do they tell us about the "real me" that we need to discover before we can honestly share ourselves with another person?

Once that quest has been satisfied, we can begin to unpeel the layers of reactions that tend to cover up our true feelings. It is said, for example, that *fear* is the root feeling which is manifested both as anger and as depression. I have discovered the truth of this in my own life experiences, very often to my great surprise, and even, on occasion, only after spending countless hours and days arguing against it. Once arriving at the realization that I had been covering up a feeling of fear, I experienced that fear so vividly that I could almost literally touch it. I could taste it and smell it. And I could describe it in such detail that another person could *feel what I was feeling*.

That is how we are called to communicate with each other in marriage, in empathy and in love. Before we can fully communicate with another, we have to *know who we are*. We don't have to know *why* we feel or react in the ways we do. But we *do* have to know *how* we feel and *how* we react—and we have to know how to communicate those feelings and reactions in such a way that *our spouse can feel our feelings.* We give these over to the one we love completely selflessly, and the gift is received in the spirit in which it is given—and it *is* a gift, no matter if the feelings soar to the heights or sink into the depths.

Commitment

I believe that the biggest deciding factor in making a relationship work is *commitment* to the relationship—and because commitment is the beginning of covenant, it is especially essential in a marital relationship. While society continues to look upon marriage as a legal "contract," covenant much more fully defines the "terms" of marriage. The Hebrew concept of covenant that has been handed down to us throughout the generations consists of five necessary parts:

- It is *God* who initiates and causes the covenant.
- We respond by *active* faith and obedience.
- The covenant is *inviolable.*
- The covenant is *steadfast* in love, kindness, justice, righteousness, fidelity, and responsibility. It is this steadfastness that allows us to never lose hope, for even should our steadfastness falter or fail we know that God's will not.
- The covenant must be *actualized* through ritual. This actualization is called "the cutting of the covenant."

God's covenant with the Jews is actualized yearly through the Passover ritual, when the people re-member the Exodus event as God's saving action for them, his Chosen People. The Christian covenant is ac-tualized daily through the Eucharist, when we re-mem-ber the body and blood of our Lord as his body, the Church. The marriage covenant is actualized each and every time a husband and wife re-member their sacra-mental character, one flesh.

Conflict Resolution

For me, conflict resolution was the most difficult of the "six Cs." We, of course, carry our individual upbringing and our personal genes into how we fight. My way is si-lence—pouting, withdrawing, feeling sorry for myself (perhaps smugly superior). My husband's way was vent-ing—cursing, blaming, dredging up the past (very vo-cally superior). Resolution was hard to come by! We each played the part of the suffering servant, but we interpreted our parts differently.

The plea for legal separation because of irrecon-cilable differences usually comes about because two grown people cannot resolve their conflicts. There may be conflicts that will *never* be resolved between us, but we *can* agree to disagree—if we keep those lines of communication open. We may have to stop yelling long enough to listen, and our spouse may have to feebly verbalize the feelings that are swirling around inside his or her head. It's a big first step in the pro-cess: from listening to each other to really hearing each other to doing whatever it takes to reach a resolution that both of us can live with.

The importance of forgiveness and reconciliation cannot be over-emphasized when we speak of this subject. It is within the intimacy of the marriage bond that persons most fully learn the meaning of forgiveness and reconciliation, for no conflict is ever fully resolved until those two demands are met.

Forgiveness has been interpreted in many ways, most of them insufficient. It is not enough, for example, to mumble a quick, "I'm sorry," and expect reconciliation. The primary reason why this is not enough is because the "penitent" is not relinquishing control of the situation over to the one who must forgive. What's a person to say to, "I'm sorry"? But if the penitent one asks forgiveness of the other, the roles have reversed. The "power" to forgive—or not to forgive—lies squarely in the hands of the wronged individual; the one who seeks forgiveness is at the mercy of the very person he or she has sinned against. "Whatever you bind on earth will be bound in heaven, and whatever you loose on earth will be loosed in heaven" (Matthew 18:18bc).

Neither is it enough to "forgive, but not forget." That, in fact, was an ongoing subject for conflict in our marriage. The "problem" is that, in not forgetting, we are not letting it go—and when we do not let it go, it continues to eat at us. That is how we come to accumulate stamp books, and in the throes of a conflict, cash them in: "What about the time you did..." or, "That is what you always say..." or something along those lines. It is rehashing things that had presumably already been forgiven. In truth, there was no forgiveness if there is still a grudge; the indiscretion of the past has not been forgotten.

To forget, in this sense of the word, doesn't mean that the *mind* has no recollection of it, as in amnesia, but that the *heart* has no recollection of it. It is what we hold in our hearts that determines our feelings and guides our actions. A person who is unforgiving hardens his or her heart. With a heart full of love and compassion and mercy, there is no room for grudges.

Mention must also be made of *the most recurrent problem* in this area of forgiveness: the lack of mercy that we show to ourselves. There can be no reconciliation between us, even if our spouse has truly forgiven us, as long as we hold on to the sin in our hearts: "I am such a failure…so bad…so unloving…so unworthy….How *can* my spouse forgive me? How, even, can *God* forgive me?" We disbelieve the forgiveness that is ours because we have not forgiven ourselves—and unless or until we do, we are effectively separated, shut off from the love that we so badly want and need.

Children

Children change our lives, radically and permanently. Children challenge the marriage relationship, even in the strongest of marriages. Once a child enters our lives, we will never again be just the two of us. Even after they have grown up and moved away, they impact our "coupleness."

The biggest immediate change is the restriction on our time for each other. That is often the cause of the first real disillusionment within a marriage. The husband may find himself feeling second-best in the affections of his wife, who is suddenly lavishing all her attentions on this new little member of the family. The new mother, too, may feel resentful at the time she has to devote to this child, and may think that the duties ought to be more equitably shared.

As the child grows, he or she becomes amazingly adept at figuring out how to "play" us, one against the other, for purposes of his or her own pleasure. Letting this continue into the child's adolescence could well find us coping with a seriously delinquent son or daughter and all that entails. One certainty in such a scenario is a fractured marital relationship—or maybe *no* marital relationship.

How we tend to parent is inherited from how we ourselves were parented—and we can rest assured that our spouse's "inheritance" is going to be different from ours. And all the advance talking in the world won't eliminate differences of opinion in any given circumstance when it comes to our children. We then tend to over-"compensate" for what we judge to be our spouse's "weakness" in the child-rearing arena, for example, if he is "too strict," she becomes "too lenient." The child suffers, but the marriage usually incurs the greater harm.

With this dismal picture, why are children considered "blessings"? It's a question often asked throughout one's parenting years, and yet there is the realization that they *are* blessings even in the worst of times. They are blessings, first of all, because they personify the love of a man and a woman, and they extend that personification beyond their parents' lifetimes. My late husband continues to live in the four children we parented together. Only children can do that. In me, he does not live on, save in memory; in them, he is both visible and audible. They carry his baggage, along with mine.

There are many other blessings, of course, and one of the greatest is living "to see your children's children." This was a blessing in disguise when I first laid eyes on my first grandchild, for I was resistant to becoming "grandma" at an age when many nowadays are just becoming parents. But in him lives my son, and in my son lives my husband, and in my husband lived his father, and the heritage continues down through the ages.

And it isn't all one-sided. My daughter enfleshes, for me, my mother; and she tells me that her daughter enfleshes me. And moving from a parent-child relationship into a peer relationship is a joy that is filled with mystery and wonder. I am even beginning to experience an occasional reversal of roles—where my children attempt to parent me—which perhaps is preparation for what may someday materialize, as I had to parent my own parents in their later years.

Church

When we were married, it was as an interchurch couple, but we both knew that I would soon become a Catholic. I was already learning about the faith. I knew how important it was to my intended, and since my own religious upbringing had never stirred in me a religious fervor, I had no problem making the change. Catholicism seemed to "make sense"; there was an "answer" for every question. In my immaturity, I found that reassuring.

How long ago that was! And when the answers stopped and the questions started, immediately after Vatican Council II, there was no more solace in the Church for either of us. For a period of perhaps three years during that time, we saw "eye to eye" on church matters. That was, in fact, possibly our *only* area of agreement during those years!

Our own religious evolution naturally affected our children. We made our way back to church suddenly, almost impulsively, with the making of a *Marriage Encounter* weekend in 1974, and we never looked back. But our "conversion" was perhaps too late, for one of the great heartaches in both our lives has been watching so many of our grandchildren grow up unchurched, some even unbaptized. And the responsibility that we bear in that weighs heavy.

Church impacts everything, and often when you least expect it. It will play a bigger and bigger part in your marriage as your family grows, because even people who are themselves unchurched seem to feel a compulsion to get some kind of "churching" for their children. What kind? If you are an interchurch or an interfaith couple, what will you do for your children's faith education? Is one of you more "religious" than the other? Is one of you more ignorant of your faith than the other? Is one of you willing to "compromise" your beliefs for the beliefs of the other?

Career

At this point in my life, I talk about my "former lives" only partly in jest. It seems as if I have, indeed, lived many lives, and still have a couple to go, God willing. And the defining of these "different lives" generally falls under the heading of "career." Which leads me to conclude, first of all, that a "career" is not a lifelong commitment. It *isn't* a vocation.

But whatever role one plays along the way, whatever thing we do to earn a living or to earn some self-respect or good feelings or whatever, obviously is an important part of our marital relationship. It may be what or who we are known as outside the home, but within the home it is merely when we are gone and what our spouse's mood is when we return. It isn't something we should "bring home" with us.

On the other hand, what we do away from home *is* a part of who we are, and we should feel free to share that part of self with our spouse. We should expect such sharing to be received with love and empathy. And we should expect the input and the support of our spouse in making and living career decisions.

Whether we like it or not, most of us are going to have to work until we're pushing 70. Whether that work is considered our career or just a job, and whether it provides stability for forty years or we find ourselves moving from company to company and city to city every few years, it is vitally important that we enjoy what we are doing. This is going to necessarily occupy the majority of our time. In order for that precious time that we have for each other to continue to flourish and grow, we must make the most of every moment.

My husband didn't enjoy any of his many jobs throughout our marriage. He counted the days till he could retire. He impressed upon our children an image of job as drudgery. Because the job absorbs so much of one's time, he was basically never very happy. His unhappiness at the office came home with him, made him edgy, gave him excuses for unhealthy behaviors. He took early retirement, but things have a way of catching up with us when our lifestyle is found wanting. He found just a few months of enjoyment before falling ill, and died at 62.

Remembrance

Nobody really wanted to come together in the "same old way" that would be so decidedly different after my husband died, but neither did anyone want to *not* carry on the tradition. Right down to the wire I went, that first year, before finally deciding to carry through on what we had "always" done. My only concession was to buy ready-made deli trays rather than spend two days cooking and slicing and laying out endless trays of food for a "help yourself" dinner that would accommodate the twenty-plus kids and grand kids who invade the house on Christmas day.

The second year was better. It was a given that we would gather, but my mother-in-law stayed away. The family stories that always permeate these special gatherings did not generate tears or melancholy, as they had the year before. My own grief had come to an end earlier in the year, as I experienced "closure" through a family prayer ritual and blessing ceremony at the grave site on my husband's birthday. Everyone even seemed to be adjusted to the "deli-ready" food.

The third Christmas was not "typical" in any sense. It was spent in a nursing home with my mother-in-law, who had been in the hospital since the day before Thanksgiving and would ultimately die on Easter Sunday—fully encompassing the holiday season for that year. We all went to her, and tried our best to make a festive day of it, but sometimes our best isn't good enough. My husband's absence was glaringly apparent that year, and on Holy Thursday I yelled at him: "Do something, will you! She's *your* mother! We can't do this anymore!"

He did. His mother spent the next two days in a comatose tomb, and on the third day—Easter Sunday—she passed to new life.

This past Christmas—my fourth one as a single—was perhaps the model for what will be "normal" in the years ahead. Everyone who could come, came, the food was a combination of deli and homemade, the enjoyment of each other was genuine, some of the family stories were even new ones, and the laughter was often raucous. And when it was time for us to think about calling it "a day," we weren't yet ready to let it go, so—as in Christmases past—we broke out a board-game and played into the wee hours of the second day of Christmas.

What does this have to do with the sacrament of marriage? For starters, it is testimony to family, which is one of the two pillars of marriage in the Church. My family is far from ideal, and its individual members far from holding all the others in a mutuality of love and respect. But on this special day, they've put aside grudges and grievances. My family is far from religious, and its individual members range from unbaptized and un-churched to semi-regular Mass-goers. But on this special day there is a trickle of accompaniment for me at the Midnight Mass or the Mass During the Day. My family is far from "conventional." But all of my children are at least legally married and none of them show any signs of separation or divorce.

It seems to me that here also is testimony to the mutual love and respect that form the first of the two pillars of marriage in the Church. My children respect the relationship that their father and I had, despite its flaws, and honor that bond in continuing to be solicitous and concerned about me and my new way of life.

The Primacy of Persons

Communication jargon is not the answer to our crises of communication, and theological jargon is not the answer to our crises of vocation. It isn't enough to talk *about* communication, or to talk around it by homing in on this or that aspect, or this or that personality type. Communication is essential for continuing growth in understanding and love. And it isn't enough to say that marriage is a sacrament and leave it to you to figure out what that means. It isn't enough to rely on old and faulty theological thought to convey the meaning and purpose of marriage.

It isn't even enough to point out that the theology has changed and marriage has become a more respected vocation in the Church than it used to be. Only *applied* theology gives witness to the truth of unique oneness that is the crowning glory of the marital sacrament. *We must live it.* We must live the sacrament for ourselves…and for our children…and for our children's children.

So talk about your expectations and your feelings *now,* listen to your beloved's expectations and feelings *now,* discuss discrepancies and possible solutions, maybe even "experiment" with two or more of those suggested solutions, and—faithfully and consistently—pray together. The important thing to keep in mind is that *nothing* is more important than your relationship and *no thing* is more important than your beloved.

As God's chosen ones, holy and beloved, clothe yourselves with compassion, kindness, humility, meekness, and patience. Bear with one another and, if anyone has a complaint against another, forgive each other; just as the Lord has forgiven you, so you also must forgive. Above all, clothe yourselves with love, which binds everything together in perfect harmony. And let the peace of Christ rule in your hearts, to which indeed you were called in the one body. And be thankful. Let the word of Christ dwell in you richly; teach and admonish one another in all wisdom; and with gratitude in your hearts sing psalms, hymns, and spiritual songs to God. And whatever you do, in word or deed, do everything in the name of the Lord Jesus, giving thanks to God the Father through him.

Colossians 3:12-15

PART II

THE WEDDING DOWRY

My Personal Baggage

When we fall in love, we have eyes only for each other. We want only to be together, to drink in the beauty and goodness of the other *so deeply that it makes each of us a new creation and the two of us one.* And this is truly sacrament. There is no greater sign of God's love than the perfect love of two people. The mystery of that perfect love defies description, and so becomes an apt description of Christ's love for his Church. We truly and joyfully would give our life for our beloved, and in many ways, we do. It is a love so deep within us that the beloved is never out of our mind. Our lover is in our every prayer. We close our eyes and see his face, feel his touch, hear his voice, smell his sweetness, and taste his lips. Our beloved is one with us.

That is why we have a sacrament of marriage. Such a perfect love is bursting at the seams to be shared. We want to "tell the world" that we're in love; we want the world to glory in our love, to feel the faith and the hope that we feel in one another. We want the world to "be in love" with our love. And so we call the world to come and witness a ritual that makes our love public: we "cut a covenant." We marry each other before the altar of God and the Church's clerical witness, and before family and friends, and that marriage is a sign—a sacrament—of Christ's love for his Church.

Many couples live together without the blessings of marriage and offer up the lame excuse that they "love" each other, that a "piece of paper" doesn't make any difference. Many have even "better" excuses: they don't believe in God, or one of them does and the other one doesn't, or they "can't afford" to get married. If you are in such a situation, ask yourself this question—and answer it honestly: If my "significant other" is killed in an automobile accident tomorrow, or simply ups and walks out on me next week, will I tell those I meet later in life that I have been married? The level of intimacy should equal *only* the level of commitment.

The passage from Colossians with which we ended part one is often read at weddings, and well it should be for it is a very apt description of sacrament and beatitude. It is, in fact, a very apt description of love that is consciously and deliberately chosen. It is a concise blueprint for Christian living.

Difficult as such an ideal life is in our world, an ideal life that is shared by two people in the most intimate of human relationships is even more difficult. Conversely, blessed as such an ideal life is in our world, an ideal life that is shared by two people in the most intimate of human relationships is doubly blessed. And the difficulties can be significantly lessened if we are aware of potential weak spots and willing to work through them.

Those potential weak spots can be traced through our genealogical roots. These roots encompass much more than your basic "country of origin" kind of information. A look at what could be called one's genealogical personality sheds light on their importance. Areas to examine include:

- the physical
- the emotional
- the sexual
- the spiritual
- the sacramental

Genealogy is "in" as never before, perhaps partly because so many of us feel "rootless" in our changing society. How does one trace ancestors when one's "family of origin" is splintered and broken, often lost and even nameless? If we have no family history, we have no means for making our own rational and informed family plans. The less we know of our roots, the more we risk failure in our future planning. The loss of what we currently call the "traditional" family has far-reaching ramifications.

The Physical

When two people fall in love and start fantasizing about marriage, genealogical considerations are generally limited to the plainly physical: When we have a child, will the baby have "your" eyes… "my" hair… "your" height…? The lovers see in one another great endearing marks of beauty that often are visible only to the two of them. Each dreams that favored physical attributes of the beloved will be manifested in the hoped for children to come. But there is that strange quirk of nature which often has all the boys in the family looking like their mother while all the girls look like their father, and it is especially apparent when the mother is short and slender and the father is big and brawny. And rarely does it occur to young lovers that they will not always look just as they do right now, whether in fact or in the star-struck eyes of the lover. We've all heard the one about taking a careful look at our in-law to see what our spouse will look like twenty years down the road. It's uncannily accurate.

That's the physical, or the most obvious of the physical. But, as anyone who has ever filled out a healthcare form knows, what we look like is not the most important element in our physical genealogy. That distinction belongs to our invisible genes. In this enlightened age, we still fail to recognize the importance of genealogy in our relationships. Because the marital relationship calls for an ongoing intimacy throughout one's life, it stands to reason that our genealogical makeup is going to impact that intimacy in intimate ways.

What kinds of debilitating diseases may we be inheriting, may we be passing on to our heirs or, in some cases, even to our spouse? Are there important, possibly life-altering or even death-dealing, decisions to be made here? Now we're not just talking about how our *kids* might look but how our *future* might look. Did all the men in our spouse's family die young with cancer? Is there a history of diabetes on our mother's side? Heart disease? Crippling arthritis? Or what about drinking problems or drug addictions? That too is the physical, tendencies that we carry in our genes and that manifest themselves with great regularity as we go through life.

Do we have a physical personality? Well, there are the athletic types, the computer nerd types, the health freak types; there are those who never sit still and those who never stand when they can sit; there are those who are so weight-conscious that they're anorexic and those who seem to gain weight just by smelling food. These are physical personalities, and some of them don't mix.

The Emotional

What kind of emotional baggage do we tote around with us, and how does it mesh with the love of our life? Ethnic roots often play a big part in this genealogical quirk of nature because our emotions are displayed as character traits and our character traits are passed down, generation unto generation. It's not for nothing that Germans are known as stoic and unfeeling, or that the Irish are known to revel in moroseness. (Trust me, born of German roots and married to an Irishman!) If you keep all your feelings to yourself and your beloved has never had an unspoken thought, trouble is brewing. If you burst into tears at the slightest provocation and your beloved is a practical joker, who's laughing? Or if you can't keep your hands off his beautiful body and he avoids even holding hands in public, who's feeling unloved?

Some emotional personalities are easy to spot, like the braggart or the whiner. These would presumably be easy types to stay away from, but people still find themselves married to such unpleasant personalities. Others are less obvious, or even seen as desirable when we don't have to live with them. How many of us tend to gravitate toward those with the "great sense of humor," for example—the ones who use humor as a means for avoiding anything unpleasant? Or the "easy-going" personality—the super procrastinator who never finishes anything?

This is akin to the physical, especially in the light of current understanding of emotional disturbances. Many emotional traits can be connected to a physical source, such as a chemical imbalance or a missing chromosome. It is in this area of emotional genealogy that we should look for signs of *impending* trouble, such as, drinks too much, gets angry too easily, is perpetually late, can't hold a job, can't make a decision.

Many of these "emotional dispositions" are genetic. Does his father drink too much, or throw the hammer across the room when the nail he's attempting to drive into the wall defies his efforts? Is her mother the kind who will "be late to her own funeral," or who "asks permission" of her husband before setting a date with the hairdresser? When we're in love we tend to overlook such ominous warning signs as these, to think that it will all change after marriage. And usually, it does—it gets worse!

Opposites attract. That explains, up front, why males like females and females like males. It explains, too, why girls who don't know a linebacker from a tight end gush all over the football hero and listen, enthralled, to his stories of valor on the field. But the chances of that kind of a relationship growing, or even continuing, are virtually non-existent. How long will it take before you are resentful of trying to carry on a meaningful conversation about the ethical implications of the latest scientific advances with a partner whose sole intellectual pursuit seems to be learning the stats of every player in the NFL? Is your idea of a great date visiting the art museum while he'd rather visit the bowling alley? Do you listen to the same radio stations? What about your tastes in movies? Want to spend the rest of your life watching second-rate horror flicks and the Fox Sports Network?

And our families of origin have something to tell us here too. Our genes play a part in our intelligence and in our intellectual interests. Have you compared GPA's and majors? But the intellectual encompasses more than I.Q. or education, for we're talking about the personality of intelligence. If your family is well-educated and sees a real value in everyone getting a higher education, and your sweetheart's family is filled with high school dropouts who never pick up a newspaper, let alone a book, there is a mighty bridge to gap.

A commonplace point of friction among couples is the bookworm versus the non-reader. They think differently. She cannot understand how he can possibly lose sleep just to finish a book and he doesn't fathom why she doesn't even want to hear about what he's just read! A newer and widespread phenomenon is the Internet junkie. This is especially divisive when there is no separate phone line for the computer!

And think of the implications for holiday get-togethers with the family. Whose family? What are their family traditions? Can you cheerfully spend the next thirty Christmases with his cigar-smoking uncle? Will you pout if he doesn't spend the next thirty Thanksgivings with your father the football fanatic? Which traditions will you take from each of your families, and which will you discard? What will be *your* family traditions? Before you commit yourself for the rest of your life, why not have a serious sit-down discussion on the meaning of life?

The Sexual

Are you a "morning person"? Have you ever tried to put your "best face" forward at 2 a.m. in order to impress someone special? How much of a "morning person" were you four hours later on *that* morning? Can you imagine doing that on a daily basis? Or do you plan to just go to bed when you're ready and leave your sweetie to the company of the TV? And then get awakened at 2 a.m. because he's ready to "make love"? And, speaking of making love, are you the romantic type who wants to be wooed into the mood? Not much wooing going on if you're awake under duress, is there?

This, obviously, is tied strongly to the emotions. We have well-ingrained individual emotions about things like making love—the when, where, and how of it especially. And if one's emotions are not engaged in the physicality of the act, or are negatively engaged, then the two of you are not truly "making love." It has been said that any healthy heterosexual man and woman can be sexually compatible. That is not true. It is not true of the "one night stand" and it is not true of people in love with each other.

It has also been said that the primary sex organ is the brain, but that is not true either—or at least not completely true, although the brain is really the "nerve center" of the entire person. But sexual compatibility is not about the physical or the intellectual. It is tied to one's preconceived ideas and thus to the emotions, but, at its core, a great sexual relationship is about passion, and passion is spiritual.

If a *great* sexual relationship is about passion, and passion is spiritual, there is little we can do to cultivate and continually have great sex. But a *good* sexual relationship can be had, can even sustain moments of passion here and there along the way, if you're willing to work at it. Yes, work at it. Without work, it's just copulating; with work, it can be lovemaking. And while this commingling of bodies is *not* what makes "two become one flesh," it is a vital ingredient in the mix. Our sexuality, you see, is *who we are for others*, and who we are for THE other in our life is of the utmost importance. We are sexual beings, with or without sexual intercourse.

Our sexuality, in fact, is our first point of contact with others. "He is all boy!...Such a sweet little lady!" We're attracted to our friends (and selective of them) based upon their authentic presentation of themselves to us: their sexuality. There is a "chemistry," a recognition and a bonding, between people who share much in common *and* between people who seemingly share nothing in common. This "chemistry" is sexuality—ours and theirs.

Our culture, unfortunately, equates sensuality with sexuality. We generally use our sensuality in one of two ways—we flaunt it or we suppress it (Madonna or Forrest Gump)—and we call *this* sexuality. This is as erroneous as calling intercourse "sex," a misnomer that has even made its way into modern dictionaries. Sex is gender, intercourse is lovemaking or, less than ideally, copulation.

"Tall, dark, and handsome" represented "sexy" to me when I was young, and any man who embodied these three elements caused a *sensual* reaction: My *sense* of sight "felt" his physical attributes. But if the other senses did not follow suit, the first impression was quickly abandoned. His voice, and the words he uttered, had to be music to my ears; the scent of him clean and inviting; the touch of his hand safe and scintillating; and, yes, even the taste of him—his lips sweetly intoxicating. And guess what? It never happened!

I discovered, however, that when all the other senses are inebriated with delight, the eyes are beguiled by beauty too—whether or not "tall, dark, and handsome" describes his physicality. Beauty is in the eye of the beholder, as they say—as is easily proven by those couples of whom we say, "I can't imagine what she sees in him!"

One's sensuality has to do with one's sexuality—but it isn't the whole ball of wax. If it were, my "sexy" friend, whom you find physically uninviting, would not appeal to you in *any* way. But suppose you *like* him, like his company. Think of how *many* people you enjoy being with because of their "personality"; to be sexually intimate with them has never crossed your mind. It is their *sexuality*, however, that attracts you—that attracts all their friends: how these persons understand themselves and present themselves to others, honestly and without affectations. That *is* who they are for others.

The Spiritual

There are many spiritual people in our midst who are, strictly speaking, not religious: They do not participate in any organized religion, do not discuss issues of theology or ethics, do not necessarily even profess "belief." But there is a depth to them that is somewhat transparent, a self-satisfaction, a sense of peace. They have plugged into their innermost feelings and are free from the constraints of the social realm in which they live. They are often seen as wisdom figures in a world awash with inanity, vanity, and banality.

While our spiritual genealogy would seem to be of less import these days than in previous generations, don't sell it short. Spiritual roots go deeper than their surface growth might indicate. And while the exception used to be to marry a person of a "different religion," it seems the exception nowadays is to find and fall in love with someone who shares our faith. It may be easier to find and fall in love with someone who professes *no* faith, who doesn't go to church or synagogue or mosque and has no intentions of ever doing so. What about this person's family? Was he or she raised a heathen? If not, your friend probably isn't one at heart—but what if he was?…what if she is? What impact will that have on your relationship? What difference will it make in the lives of your future children?

Or what if you really do share the same "religion": you're both Catholic, or you're both Methodist, or you're both Jewish? Watch out, this may be the most volatile of all combinations! We are much better at ecumenism between faiths than we are within faiths! One of the great fallacies of life is that when we share a "common" faith, there will be no religion problems.

My husband was happy when I decided to convert to his faith; he thought we'd be forevermore on the same spiritual wavelength. But he was *very* wrong because I became *very* serious about this momentous change in my life. As he later put it, "She got so religious it almost made me sick!" When I wanted to get up early and go to church while my husband wanted to "sleep in," there were arguments. Even settling for each of us doing what we wanted didn't solve the problem, because we resented each other's decision. And we disagreed with each other's reasoning. Imagine how many fights we got into after I decided to get a degree in theology and tried out my newly discovered "faith facts" on him!

There is a widespread misconception of what spirituality means. One's spirituality involves much more than what one believes, or how one prays, or whether or how often one goes to church. Our spirituality is not about what we do. If our sexuality is who we are for others, our spirituality is *who we are for ourselves*. Our spirituality is our relationship with our inner being, our core, wherein resides the very Spirit of God. While our sexuality encompasses our personality, our public persona, our spirituality encompasses our being. It is the very essence of who we are at root: our soul. A person who has never explored his or her depth of being is one who is not spiritual, regardless of whether that person is "religious" or not. Victor Hugo wrote, "To love another person is to see the face of God." When we can share who we are, at our core, with another person, we truly see the face of God reflected back to us.

The Sacramental

The sacramental is *who we are for God*, for when we are a sacramental people we are signs of God: we are being who we are called to be from our mother's womb by a Creator who lovingly formed and fashioned us in the divine image. Our sacramentality does not consist of how many sacraments we have "received," but of how we manifest the God whose we are to others. Thus does the "sacrament" of marriage happen over and over, and thus does it often take years to happen with any consistency. Thus too, unfortunately, is it often the case that no sacrament of marriage ever happens, with or without benefit of a "church" wedding.

Sacraments, in other words, are not merely "received" at the hands of a bishop, priest, deacon, or spouse; they are not something we "get." Sacraments are "given," from the core of our being, when we plumb the depths of whose we are and manifest that reality to those with whom we come in contact. Briefly, then, a look at "the seven sacraments" of the Church.

In *baptism*, we become a member of a "house church," a parish community that vows its acceptance of us and its allegiance to us. In infant baptism, this choice of community is made by others; as a catechumen, we make the choice for ourselves. Either way, it is the community of believers that models the sacrament for us. Our "reception" of baptism signifies that *we will follow*: We will learn from the community to which we have been attached, and we will manifest the God in whose name we were received to others. Baptism is our initiation into the larger family, our introduction to the communal life.

In *confirmation*, we become a member of a "local church," a community that includes many house churches and their communities, and that willingly links hands and hearts for the common good of all. Our "reception" of confirmation signifies that *we will imitate*: We will work with the community to which we are attached, and we will "be Christ" for others. Confirmation is our initiation into the particular community, our invitation to love our neighbor as our self, to serve rather than to be served..

Eucharist unites us with the universal body of Christ. Whenever we receive the bread and the wine *with full faith in Christ's Real Presence*, we are also fully aware of that awesome connection and the challenge that comes with it: *We are Christ*, in and for the world in which we live; *we are sacrament*, incarnate sign of God, doing all these things, and greater things still (John 14:12) because we encompass the whole world and so can reach its farthest limits with the divine compassion embodied in us. Eucharist is our ongoing food for the journey.

Reconciliation keeps us one with each other and with

God, for we all know how easy it is to cut ourselves off. We get our feelings hurt and silently sulk, or get angry and make loud accusations or lame self-defenses; we make judgments about another's behavior or way of life or overall appearance and discount that one's value; we suffer injustice and blame another, even God, for it. We even become self-indulgent and self-righteous to the point of demanding, or at least condoning, the violent taking of human life in acts of abortion and euthanasia, capital punishment, revenge and war, physical and sexual abuse, and road rage. Only sincere repentance and acts of penitence can heal us; only reconciliation can restore the community and bring us back into the wholeness of the body. And when we are so touched by God's grace that we seek such reconciliation, *we are sacrament*, incarnate sign of the God who forgives us just as we forgive.

The *anointing of the sick* is salve for the body just as reconciliation is salve for the heart. When we are anointed, we feel loved and protected; often, we even feel a surge of strength returning to a sick or dying body. We know that we are not alone, that we need not be consumed by the pain or afraid of the future. Mary of Bethany anointed Jesus with her own consoling tears and the gentle touch of her hair (John 12:3). Jesus anointed his friends at the Last Supper with cleansing water and a towel warmed by his own body (John 13:5). When we pray with and for another person, touching that person with loving care, perhaps gently applying a soothing lotion to dry skin or a cool compress to a hot brow, we anoint that person with our love; *we are sacrament*, incarnate sign of God's healing touch.

Set apart as a sacrament by the Church is *orders*, or ordination, which is humanly limited to men and translates into bishops, priests, and deacons. Left out of this definition are others who take vows to dedicate their lives to Christ in ministry, those known as religious brothers and sisters, and monks (who do not perform priestly duties) and nuns. Bishops, priests, and deacons are to be signs of God in the world. The definition says that "conferral of the sacrament" on these men gives them a kind of exclusive power that the rest of us do not have—the power, for example, to "confer" those other sacraments, named above, on us.

Yet each of us is called to be "priest, prophet, and king," and it is only when we are, in fact, *being those*, that Christ is incarnated in our world. *And that is what sacrament means.* So the ordained man who is priest, prophet, and king for us is a *living sacrament*, and the works to which he dedicates himself are *sacramental* works. But without us he has no exclusive power, for it is in and through the community that Christ is Really Present and it is in and through the power of the Holy Spirit that ordinary substances like bread and wine can become extraordinary gifts of body and blood given for the world—the "power" of orders resides in God and in the community God gathers.

Thus do we come to *marriage*, the last sacrament to be fully defined by the Church and the only sacrament that is *not* "conferred" by an ordained representative of the Church. That ordained representative *witnesses*—for the whole universal body of Christ—the sacrament that the man and woman *confer upon each other*. The Church recognizes that marriage is unique and uniquely "ordered," a recognition that precedes the time of its being named a sacrament, for couples in the Church had to do nothing more than declare their desire to marry and vow their faithfulness to one another in order to be married. And the definition is true.

After this the Lord appointed seventy others and sent them on ahead of him in pairs to every town and place where he himself intended to go. He said to them, "The harvest is plentiful, but the laborers are few; therefore ask the Lord of the harvest to send out laborers into his harvest. Go on your way. See, I am sending you out like lambs into the midst of wolves. Carry no purse, no bag, no sandals; and greet no one on the road. Whatever house you enter, first say, 'Peace to this house!' And if anyone is there who shares in peace, your peace will rest on that person; but if not, it will return to you. Remain in the same house, eating and drinking whatever they provide, for the laborer deserves to be paid. Do not move about from house to house. Whenever you enter a town and its people welcome you, eat what is set before you; cure the sick who are there, and say to them, 'The kingdom of God has come near to you.' But whenever you enter a town and they do not welcome you, go out into its streets and say, 'Even the dust of your town that clings to our feet, we wipe off in protest against you. Yet know this: the kingdom of God has come near.'"

Luke 10:1-11

PART III

THE MARRIAGE COVENANT

Two Become One

Have you not read that the one who made them at the beginning "made them male and female," and said, "For this reason a man shall leave his father and mother and be joined to his wife, and the two shall become one flesh"? So they are no longer two, but one flesh. Therefore what God has joined together, let no one separate.

Matthew 19:4-6

What *makes* marriage a sacrament? It isn't that the wedding happens in a church. It isn't even because of that famous scriptural passage about God joining us together. No. The only parties responsible for making marriage a sacrament are *the husband and the wife* who, together, make the love of God visible and active in this world.

The indissoluble character of marriage is rooted in Scripture, but it was first presented as a sacrament late in the fourth century by Saint Augustine in a response to the heresy of Manichaeism. Augustine said marriage was good for three reasons: fidelity, which means that "one avoids all sexual activity apart from one's marriage"; offspring, which means that "the child is accepted in love, nurtured in affection, brought up in religion"; and sacrament, which means that "the marriage is not severed nor the spouse abandoned."

Augustine called marriage a "sacrament of permanence," and said it was this that distinguished Christian marriage from the marriages of non-Christians. But it was *baptism* that was permanent, so Augustine was saying that baptized persons who married were likewise permanently married. It was this analogizing of marriage to baptism that set the stage for a "defined" Church doctrine of a Christ-instituted indissoluble sacrament of marriage—although that didn't actually happen until the Council of Trent in 1549.

The 1917 Code used the same baptism/marriage/sacrament formula, basically unchanged from the time of Augustine and into the present. But if "the sacrament of matrimony presupposes and demands faith" (according to the Rite of Marriage), are those baptized who lack faith *capable* of giving and receiving the sacrament? Or are we to believe that every validly baptized Christian has faith? It is difficult to imagine that even Church teaching would make such a claim as that! This is the crux of the matter, the question that must be addressed, regardless of what words church law uses.

The document of the Second Vatican Council on "The Church in the Modern World," *Gaudium et spes*, speaks of marriage as an intimate sharing of married life

and love, a concept far removed from the coldly imper-
sonal 1917 Code of Canon Law, which included:

- Canon 1013, no. 1—The primary end of marriage is the procreation and education of children; the secondary, mutual assistance and the
  remedy of concupiscence.
- Canon 1081, no. 2—The object of marital con-
  sent is the perpetual and exclusive right to the
  body for acts which are per se to generate offspring.

The documents of the Second Vatican Council re-
sulted in a revised Code of Canon Law, promulgated in
1983, which redefined marriage's object and end:

- Canon 1005, no. 1—The matrimonial covenant, by which a man and a woman establish
  between themselves a partnership of the whole
  of life and which is ordered by its nature to the
  good of the spouses and the procreation and
  education of offspring, has been raised by
  Christ the Lord to the dignity of a sacrament
  between the baptized.
- Canon 1005, no. 2—For this reason, a valid
  matrimonial contract cannot exist between the
  baptized without it being by that fact a sacrament.

Altogether, there are one hundred eleven canons on
marriage in the 1983 Code, which speaks to the mind-set

of ecclesial authority. No other subject in the Code is so heavily weighed down. And, despite the sheer bulk of material here, it fails to adequately address marriage because "law" is not concerned with what "two become one" means. Marriage has to do with sharing life in all its extremes, the intimacies and the alienations. It has to do with respectful and attentive presence, with humble vulnerability, with self-giving and selfless receiving.

Jesuit theologian Karl Rahner, in presenting a theology of sacramental love, speaks of "love of desire" and "love of generosity" as two coexisting and active poles. The lover greatly desires the beloved as the cradle of chaste completion, while at the same time wanting only genuine good for the beloved regardless of the "cost" to the lover. From the Greek, these two poles of love would be *eros*, love for one's own pleasure, and *agape*, sometimes referred to as "unconditional love" because it is love for the sake of the other—no strings attached. To these must be added a third pole, the love called *philia*— friendship—for without friendship there can be no *agape*, and without friendship *eros* will soon burn out. It is this trinity of loving that makes a sacrament of a marriage, sign of God's infinite love. *This* is sacramental marriage.

So we have more than a difference in semantics when we seek to define marriage as a sacrament. We have a difference in faith, a difference in belief: grace versus with-strings, or reality versus law, or mystery versus definition, or—plain and simple—covenant versus contract. As anyone who has ever experienced divine mystery knows, language cannot adequately describe it, and language certainly cannot adequately define it. And the reality of a sacramental relationship is that it *is* mystery, it *is* covenant, it *is* pure and divine gift.

Needless to say, there are many marriages that do not betray this sacramentality to the world. The reason is that they are *not* sacramental marriages, regardless of where the ritual ceremony may have taken place. The ritual does not the sacrament make, certainly no more in marriage than in any of the other sacraments of the Church. God is not incarnated through a ritual; God is incarnated through people.

One Flesh

According to Scripture, in marriage we become "one flesh." This is more than physical intercourse, despite the fact that the Church used to refer to that act as the "consummation" of the marriage. People have intercourse all the time nowadays, but that doesn't make them "one flesh." They have intercourse with more than one partner. Can they be "one flesh" with multiple others? To be "one flesh" means that we love each other "for better or for worse, for richer or for poorer, in sickness and in health, until death."

As with *all* the sacraments, in marriage *we are sacrament for one another*. In this most intense and intimate of human relationships, the relationship of spouses, we give our sacramental being to our beloved and, conversely, receive the sacramental being of our beloved within our own being. We "become one" uniquely, and yet analogously to how we become one with the entire community of the Church in Eucharist. And in our oneness, we uniquely manifest the sacramentality of all the other sacraments:

- We follow, feed, and imitate one another, the collective meaning of the initiation sacraments.
- We forgive, anoint, and heal one another, the unitive goal of the reconciliation and anointing sacraments.
- We minister to and empower one another, the outward mark of the sacrament of orders.
- *We are Christ for one another*, the definitive meaning of the sacrament of marriage and *the ultimate meaning of sacrament.*

It is from within this marital relationship that we *learn* to love others with the love of Christ; it begins here, in the "domestic family" that we become when we take up residence in each other's hearts and choose to occupy a common home in the fidelity of marriage. If our love is blessed to be personified by children of our loins, we introduce them to the extended family of the parish via their baptism. If our marital family has to grow through other avenues, such as adoption, these children too personify our love and are embraced by our parish house church. And if our fate is to remain a domestic family of two, in our unique Christ-like love for one another, we are still church and still members of the one body, the Church. For such is the true meaning of marriage, of two become one.

For Better or Worse

We will love each other for better or for worse. Sounds good, but that is possibly the most ambivalent statement in the standard marriage vows. Talk about uncertainty! My husband used to tell people, "I never realized how *much* 'worse' it would get!" We survived all sorts of infidelities (and adultery is neither the only *nor* necessarily the worst "infidelity") within the first eighteen years of our marriage. We survived because we believed that marriage was forever, no matter what, and if it was miserable that's just the way life was; we lived with it.

Then, midway through the very week that we were scheduled to make a marriage retreat, I made up my mind I could *not* "just live with it" anymore. After the weekend, I was going to file for divorce!

The gift of retrospection has shown me, over and over again, that when it seems all is lost, God provides a means for us to find our way back. That weekend retreat is a case in point. We were both blessed with an awakening, a realization that if we had a choice of doing it all again or not, *we would*. We *wanted* our marriage to work.

I never told my husband of that derailed decision to divorce. One of the things that weekend taught me was the difference between "openness" and "frankness": openness is honesty from the heart; frankness is factual fratricide. In openness, we began the long and rigorous task of *making a marriage*.

For Richer or Poorer

But it also got "poorer." Through those first young years, we'd had our share of scraping for pennies, stretching meals, doing without, but nothing like what we were to experience around the time of our twenty-fifth anniversary. This was a "poorer" we never imagined could happen to us! Due to circumstances beyond our control, we became a household of five adults with a combined income of three miserable unemployment checks. And we, like so many others before and since, had been living beyond our means on credit cards for years. We were staring bankruptcy in the face—just at the time when we thought everything should have been "coming up roses" for us.

But by then we had become sacrament for one another and we worked in partnership. God provided for our material needs, one by one, as they arose. Our love grew stronger, and our commitment grew deeper. And we served as role models for couples contemplating marriage, and for couples experiencing their early years of marriage, and for couples struggling in their marriage. Our love was a visible sign of the great invisible love of God in this world. We were one flesh.

And yet, we did *not* have a single identity. The more "one" we became, the more free we were to explore our *self*-identities, to become the "me" that God had in mind when our earthly lives began. Gone were all vestiges of the persons we had been in our younger days. As we grew more secure in our love for each other, we also grew more secure in who we were, more confident in what we could accomplish, more discerning in our decision-making. And what happened next is really mind-boggling: We *individually* became sacrament to others—people who knew us simply as "Jim" or simply as "Elsie," people who never met our spouse.

Our own interests and our own pursuits did not serve to sever our togetherness, to find us going our separate ways as they had in our early days, when finding things to do and places to go without the other had been a means of survival. Now we looked forward to sharing our newfound knowledge or experiences with one another, and such sharing served to further enrich us in our relationship. We still failed, of course, but we had learned to listen to each other and we had learned that when we did it was good for *both* of us. It was sacramental.

In Sickness and In Health

One thing that we tend to be totally oblivious to when we're planning marriage is the whole area of "sickness and health." Of course, most of us are healthy when we marry, and if we've never experienced any serious health problems the possibility of sickness never enters our mind. And we were certainly luckier than many, for neither of us was ever seriously ill—until my husband started bleeding and was diagnosed with cancer. From health to sickness, literally overnight; from life to death in eight agonizing months.

But eight months is a far cry from year after year of living with pain, or year after year of living with someone who is dependent upon you for the simplest of things.

My father had to care for my mother for thirteen years following a brain aneurysm, a debilitating stroke, and Parkinson's. For many, it is perhaps less intense but longer lasting, as when a young woman develops diabetes during pregnancy and it never goes away, or a young man suffers a sudden and severe heart attack and is placed on permanent disability for the rest of his life.

Or the sickness may be in a child of your marriage, or in one or another of your parents, and you suddenly find yourselves primary caregivers. What toll does this take on a marriage? Why do some couples survive, seemingly at all costs, and others collapse under the demands such stressful responsibility places on them?

The Decision to Love

A good marriage is one which allows for changes and growth in the individuals.

Pearl S. Buck

Marriage Encounter, the marriage enrichment program that saved our marriage, introduces the concepts of romance, disillusionment, and true joy as benchmarks in relationships. When we fall in love, we are obviously in the throes of romance, and this romance generally sustains us a few years into marriage. But gradually disillusionment creeps in. Another word for disillusionment might very well be reality, for the real world intrudes on our romantic liaison—the real world of stress-related living. The money doesn't stretch far enough, the time together is squeezed tighter, and the things we had found so enchanting about each other become petty annoyances.

True to our need for completeness, perhaps, most of us fall in love with someone whose strengths are our weaknesses, and we admire those strengths and come to rely on them. The introvert loves the extrovert's ability to be at ease in any situation. The slob delights to be accepted into the company of the neatnik. But what happens when this "completeness" becomes a 24/7 thing? The neatnik gets tired of picking up after the slob, the extrovert feels hampered by the constant company of the introvert, and the madly-in-love couple fall into disillusionment. "Do I have to put up with this for the rest of my life? Is this all there is to look forward to?"

Disillusionment is inevitable, and it is recurring, but it isn't all there is, for when we make the effort to rise above it—when we make a commitment—we are often surprised to find true joy. True joy encompasses both disillusionment and romance, for it offers us the gift of true love—love that is based firmly upon the reality of knowing and accepting and appreciating the real person our spouse is, warts and all. More than that, it affirms us as who we are, warts and all. We know we are loved, cherished in fact, without pretense or affectations. We feel connected, really and truly one with each other. And while we will continue to experience moments and periods of disillusionment, we will never again wallow in it because the truth of our oneness lives in us—24/7.

Once I decided to stop trying to change my husband and to accept him as he was, life was less stressful for me (and I'm sure, for him too). Once I decided to stop trying to be what I thought my husband wanted me to be, and to do what needed to be done in order to become what I felt called to be, life was more fun for me (and eventually, for him too). If he didn't want to hear about those things I found exciting, I didn't insist on telling him anyway. On the other hand, I continued to encourage him to tell me what was happening in his life away from home—to offer advice when it was asked for and to simply listen when it wasn't—and to solicit advice from him when I was faced with doing or deciding something in my life away from home.

As our individuality grew, our "coupleness" grew also. We were no longer carbon copies of each other, but complementary parts of the one body we were becoming. We were sacrament—sign of love to others. We had strangers smile and ask us if we were honeymooners. This was such a surprise to us that, after the third or fourth occurrence, we asked the stranger why she *thought* we were. We were holding hands! It was something we automatically did, for the rest of our life together, but it was true that we had *not* done it for fifteen years before the *Marriage Encounter* weekend. Now I find myself smiling at every couple who holds hands when they are in public. It is such a small thing, but it says so much. It says they are in love with each other, and it says it to the world.

We had friends tell us that they never thought of one of us without thinking of both of us. There is something wonderful in that kind of an identity. When meeting new people, we introduced ourselves as "Jim and Elsie." If we were alone, it was the same: "Hi, I'm Elsie, Jim's wife"; or "I'm Jim, married to Elsie." After his death, it was difficult for me to consciously remember that I was now *only* Elsie. My whole identity had changed, diminished. I was a different person, and that person was a stranger to me. I had to learn to know myself all over again before I could confidently introduce myself to strangers.

Our teenage son told us that he "sure was glad" we'd done that Marriage Encounter, because life at home was "sure more peaceful." And our pastor *still* speaks of the impression our "coupleness" made on him every time we received Eucharist together. After my husband was ordained a deacon and served at the altar, I felt the same sense of diminishment that I was to experience after his death. I had to receive the bread and cup alone, and it didn't seem right. His sacrament of orders was not meant to supercede his sacrament of marriage, but it put a distance between us at the very place we both loved so dearly: the table of our Savior. When I serve as eucharistic minister, I make an unspoken point of uniting couples at the eucharistic table even though they approach it singly: I do not wipe and turn the cup after one spouse has received, but deliberately hand it to the other spouse in its same position. Nothing can more powerfully assist two in becoming one than the holy Presence of Love.

Think about the Lukan sending story (page 47). Two by two, we are sent to bring life and evangelize the world, just as two by two the male and female of all species were sent into the ark in order to preserve life and repopulate the world after the flood. This emphasis on "pairs" plainly intimates male and female simply because two men would not be referred to as a pair. Luke makes it clear throughout his gospel, in parallel after parallel, that women and men together made up the contingency of Jesus' disciples. This emphasis on "pairs," in fact, may be the more fitting Scripture to reference when we speak of Jesus instituting the sacrament of marriage, for while his teaching on divorce stresses indissolubility (Matthew 6:31-32), his sending in pairs emphasizes sacramentality.

Until Death

Couples who feel called by God to have a permanent, in-dissoluble marriage covenant will need the free-flowing grace of God in their lives in order to make their marriage sacramental in nature. They should be able to say that, of their own free wills, they are making a covenant before God to love, honor, cherish, obey, and be faithful to each other until death, no matter what happens. Willingly, they agree to place each other's needs and the needs of their family before their own, to try to resolve conflicts, to support and help their spouse's relationship with Christ. In short, they are promising to love each other with God's sacrificial, unconditional love. Such a covenant before God is a sacrament, and indissoluble, as stated in Mark 10:9. In the sight of God, and with God's blessing, the Catholic Church joyously joins the bride and groom who come to the altar with these loving intentions.

Dennis & Kay Flowers[1]

---

1 Dennis and Kay Flowers, *Catholic Annulment, Spiritual Healing,* Liguori Publications, Liguori, MO, 2002, page 27.

When the risen Jesus calls Mary Magdalen by name and she recognizes her beloved, she instinctively reaches for him. But Jesus tells her, "Do not hold on to me, because I have not yet ascended to the Father" (John 20:17a). Much as we want to, we cannot hold on to those we love. They may be a part of us, a part of us may die with their leave-taking, but they never really belong to us; their presence and their love is the sheer unbridled gift of God.

I first discovered this personally when my mother was languishing in a nursing home. She wanted to die, but I wanted to hold on to her. She told me as best she could, being unable to really communicate since suffering a stroke five years earlier. I tried not to notice. One day, as I bent over to kiss her goodbye, her hand grasped at me. Her eyes pleaded with me. "Die," she whispered weakly. "Die?" I repeated. She nodded her head. "You want to die?" I asked. She nodded again. Resigned, I told her that we should both pray for that. She looked happier, and began mumbling the Lord's Prayer. I prayed it with her. It was Sunday afternoon. Finally having my "permission," she died on Tuesday morning.

When my husband was suffering, weak and feeling helpless, he would say to me, "This isn't living, Elsie. This isn't living." After he lapsed into a restless coma, I knew there was no future for us. And when, in his one moment of coherent recognition, he looked at me with a dimming light of love in his eyes and made a concerted effort to sustain his labored breathing, I heard myself saying words I was not conscious of thinking. "Oh, sweetheart, go with God!" Through the grace of God, I did not hold on to him. He closed his eyes…and stopped breathing.

We take our vows "until death." Death is inevitable, and death is difficult. We had survived the deaths of his father and both my parents. We survived losing four grandchildren to miscarriages and extrauterine pregnancies. Eventually and indubitably, only one of us will survive a marriage. The surviving spouse *cannot* prepare for life as a single because *all the rules change* and nobody knows the demands this whole new life will make of them. In my case, it was the *first time* I had ever lived alone— reason enough to lose equilibrium!

And I did…big time. But the saying is true: It is better to have loved and lost than to not have loved at all. Every love we have in this life will eventually be lost, and if it is not lost *until* death, we are indeed blessed. I believe that if we have loved well, if we have walked the path into death with our spouse, and if we allow our self the gift of healthy grief for as long as we need to grieve, we *are* given new life.

With earthly death, life has changed, not ended (see 1 Corinthians 15:51). As it is throughout our lives, *we have to choose*: life or death (see Deuteronomy 3:15-20). Then, and *only* then, is the sacrament of marriage over…and we have another saint in heaven interceding for us.